Currents

Cry. And wither within. Yet stay strong. Incredibly strong. That's what *Currents* by Bojan Louis is. Knowledge is knowledge. It is not spare. Yet, truth to tell, knowledge is spare. But it's there where it has always been. Where it belongs. Truth or fact or answer is beside the point. Reading Louis's poems, I have to stop many times. At times, I feel I lose track. But that's okay. Awareness makes sure you are current. And ready, prepared, fixated by experience. Mine, not his. That's when it hits me. Religion and religious experience is the way to Phoenix from Las Vegas. We'll get there, and we'll be ready. Make sure you read the notes at the end of Bojan's book of poems, which tell you more than you know and swear by.

—Simon J. Ortiz, *From Sand Creek, Out There Somewhere, Beyond the Reach of Time and Change* (ed.)

Currents
POEMS

BOJAN LOUIS

BkMk Press
University of Missouri-Kansas City
www.umkc.edu/bkmk

BkMk Press
University of Missouri-Kansas City
5101 Rockhill Road
Kansas City, MO 64110
www.umkc.edu/bkmk

Executive Editor: Robert Stewart
Managing Editor: Ben Furnish
Assistant Managing Editor: Cynthia Beard
Cover art: Gary Louis (Askilchii)
Technical consultant: Sherwin Bitsui

BkMk Press wishes to thank Dana Sanginari, Barbara Magiera, McKensie
Callahan, and Josiah Pabst. Special thanks to Serna Dobson.

Financial assistance for this book has been provided by the Missouri Arts
Council, a state agency. Additional assistance has been provided by the Miller-
Mellor Foundation.

Library of Congress Cataloging-in-Publication Data

Names: Louis, Bojan, author.
Title: Currents / Bojan Louis.
Description: First edition. | Kansas City, MO : BkMk Press/University of
    Missouri-Kansas City, [2017] | Includes bibliographical references.
Identifiers: LCCN 2017025081 | ISBN 9781943491117 (softcover : acid -free
    paper)
Classification: LCC PS3612.O789 A6 2017 | DDC 811/.6--dc23 LC record
available at https://lccn.loc.gov/2017025081

ISBN: 978-1-943491-11-7

for

shimá sání,

my family,

&

Sara Sams

Acknowledgments

Grateful acknowledgement is made to the editors of the following journals in which some of these poems first appeared: *Matter: A (somewhat) monthly journal of political poetry and commentary*: "If Nothing, the Land"; *Permafrost*: "There" and "*Bini' Anit'ą́ą́ Ts'ósí*"; *Black Renaissance Noire*: "Arc Flash," "Middle of the Desert," "Breach," "This Side of the River," "*Ko' dóó łeesch'iih*"; *American Indian Culture and Research Journal*: "Troubleshooting," "One's Own," "A Structure in Parts," and "Hydrolysis"; *Hinchas de Poesía*: "Division," "Grounding," "*Hwéeldi*"; *Platte Valley Review*: "Currents"; *Kenyon Review*: "Baptism for the Dead," "Red Dirt," "Electricity."

Special thanks to Cynthia Hogue and the Modernism class where the initial seeds and realization of this collection began so many years ago; to Stuart Dybek for his support, advice, and friendship; to the mighty Simon J. Ortiz for pulling me out of concussion and darkness and pushing me ever forward; to Diné poets Orlando White and Sherwin Bitsui. Also, to the MacDowell Colony for the time and support in order to further realize and shape this collection alongside the short fiction I was there to write; and to the friends of that residency for their sincerity and genius.

All gratitude and love to my mother, Nora Louis, for being a model of strength and perseverance, and to my father, Gary Louis, for his art and love, and to my sister, whom I love greatly; the Diné Nation and all my family; Roy Louis for all the "recharges"; my crew of humanist rabble-rousers: Kendall and Carrie Ann Vesica Piscis, "Metal" Joe Karlin, Bryan "Spanky" Stewart, Gup (RIP), Shomit Baura, Fernando Pérez, Cruz Pérez 2.0, David Antonio Moody, Mark and Kelly Haunschild, Henry Quintero, Bill Wetzel, and Lauren Espinoza; to Philadelphia poets Paul Siegell and Ernest Hilbert for helping me survive and thrive during my time there and to the Indigenous transplants I found lurking there; my new Tennessee family for being "so Ridge"; my friends in Logroño, Madrid, and Barcelona; and all my dogs past and present: Shasha, Coconino, Coba, Mega, and Lorca.

And to Sara Sams. Life partner in crime and in light.

Contents

Breach

Sitka, Alaska

I.

It's years I've been recovered.
Parents gone the way of worms
—Mom alone, her own decision.

Dad, how he was always
asphyxiated until rolled over.
The frontier I'm abandoned to,

exposed root ribcages above ground,
rained on so much there's no dust,
no blow away—traceless surfaces.

With a single bag and one-way ticket
I rented the first found available:
three bedroom, living, kitchen, dining

—filled it with myself, every room
empty, except where I slept.
Girls I had over, fucked to the floor,

left sobered, mostly. Offered other
times at their places later. I accepted,
then abandoned, fixed at the clinic.

This high north, though not freezing,
an island settlement cut off the coast:
pines, spruce, and chaotic undergrowth

rise up along the crescent of mountains
open toward the ocean.
Rain more sky than the sky is sky.

I'm not home. Less
interested in finding it;
hours from the mainland.

II.

On an outlying island red deer
wait out hunters tracking
shit steam for rifle crack.

Otters cut away
supine through water,
to humans hypothermic.

The turned-engine skiff
on sucking mud signals
the goddamned day's done.

———

Across the still, cobalt inlet,
cairns line the bald rim
of a sundowner volcano.

Glaciers imagined against
the sea/heaven horizon
melt when fog lifts

and missed shots echo,
fade into the tree line:
the casings mimic pebbles.

———

Anger defines me, here,
in what's seen in pictures
as pristine beauty, untouched

by man's dirty finger:
Dad's belched regrets,
Mom's frustrated, unspoken hurt.

I want recompense—solitude
and forgiveness' distance—nourishment
sought, sighted, and put down.

III.

Where welding fails
release hollers out the soon-
to-be-empty space.

A continent,
a levee. What
rises, takes

—ice given heat,
like a child, spread
with hands telling, quiet.

———

Ocean hefted over stern
deflates
my ill posture

gone life-drunk;
so drowned in drink
nobody wants to want me.

Rare are dads shouted
at by moms, Get—Don't feed
us—Sink, be eaten.

———

Jonah's a lucky fuck,
bowel-held
and undigested.

Dumb animal, him. Swallowed
entire, in warmer water.
I don't believe he escaped.

He's down in there still.
Hung from the beast's spine,
feet eaten, body untouched.

Prayer

I.

My system is ruined
by foreign pathogens
blooming.

I call it, more
or less, blood

created for me. Creator,
should I call it you?

II.

I don't dream
or rest.

On this exhausted circuit
I'm in pursuit: better

to forget, *keep trying*.
Do, simply, until done.

III.

There's no water
here, but life is.

Sun and moon thread
this ground.

The walk,
the weaving.

IV.

If I get another life,
complaints will be missing.

Fused phases arcing,
sudden and temporary

—sound bites
for short films.

Ko' dóó Łeeschch'iih

The red off the far ridge, an eating dragon, slow
      coming down the valley
—my mom's imagination over the phone,
      a quarter-mile of cars ahead.

No one has stopped, on their way north or south,
to capture Hotshots turning the beast to smolder.

Somewhere out in the burn, under dusk, a rattler
      den unfurls fast as brush fire
and clenches against the inferno draft
      that blocks entrance and escape.

For an instant, or minutes maybe, their unnatural
warmth is a comfort beneath the ablaze final day.

It's the shape I'm in. I don't tell her that I will
      leave, days from this moment,
the high, dry mountain we drive toward
      for the ashes of a different monster.

Hydrolysis

Coal Mine Mesa, Navajo Nation

I.

To hunt work down, her dad slurred
as consistently as the days
his unemployment was condoned.

No mail delivery or landlines she hitched,
anytime the neighbor's wagon passed.
Funny. In the '50s, most the country drove.

Had busses stopping at the long end of dirt
ruts. Wouldn't have mattered.
Liver failure, dysentery would keep him home.

———

Before ever playing with books and paper
my mother swung axes.
Kindling, priority over that of her heart's.

The hope for supper and frosted-dune
dawns indebted the family
to wood. She and her siblings stole

what made stars burn from gas cans
at the trading post
and huffed that shit into their lungs.

———

It's neat to scissor perforated outlines,
so that the cut keeps—
feathered edges thirst for moisture,

dissolve, and warble like voices
nixing sleep.
Somnambulant sons and daughters

cleaved from the everyday bonding
of their parents.
If it's not them who alter, it's *you*.

II.

It's *knock-up* when solar hues dampen
the trek home's frost
after a desperate and smitten beau,

whose bed is already shared by a sibling,
swears palm to chest
that his groin is sated, no longer a trope

of want or population. But a tropic
above the equator, where
one heat is necessary, one heat is good.

———

Handouts buy diapers hardly, ever. Do food,
sometimes. A belly,
stretch-marked and loose, after a body's exit

is again a plasterer's hawk, a temporary
hold before a more permanent
smearing. Lead paint bleeding into asbestos,

crumbling to flake and dust. An interlock
of detritus, dead weeds
blown against volcanic rock. Birth to birth, all this.

———

Off the uranium-wind reservation, on Utah farms
and in cities, god comes easy;
a touching that's domestic, the fault of being

language-naughty or sun-darkened pretty;
simple as thighs
like chicken skin, pussy wet like dog nose.

A truth that is contraband distributed
on the home front, where
the more you lose yourself, the less is asked of you.

III.

It's better if monsters are vanquished with *our* stories.
Done in by Hero Twins:
Naayéé'neizghání dóó Tóbájíshchíní. Mom's words

—labyrinths aren't nature's making, humans
obsessed over harnessing
a pattern; placing dead ends, calling walls art.

Whether trimmed hedge or bonded by mortar
both, anything really, began
in water. And it keeps us, and it keeps us.

———

Despite my traditional knowing, there's no other
being I'll see in the poorly
stained cedar cabinet willed to me. A Greek

he-monster. Myth trim and fit with afflictions
of earth. Moss beard, stump horns,
hoof foot, and lichen plaque. Not an ideal.

More a reject that science or the pope will heal.
It's not a matter of what I see.
After a burial, the unstained cedar can be burned.

———

Time, in any circumstance, disfigures. Basically,
don't be bothered by what
you can't know. Keep at that bucolic dream.

The one where money is no problem but
something else is, like
sky without bird, gust with no pollen, or

season with one temperature.
A place where wind never quits,
just blows some other way.

This Side of the River

i.

Five years in
my wolf/husky
is poisoned

by an older boy
who'll turn vegetable
after head trauma.

I'll smell him, bodied by a horse
run loose on a no-moon roadway
from Window Rock to Crystal,

fold my small body and
leave memories of being
fondled in the bathroom unlit;

choked until I complied
to perform naked
with the sitter

for the neighbor—
three-tiered event:
voyeur, participant, watched.

ii.

Only in five years,
it's hard to believe
that you were placed
in your mother's body
—given and given
to this earth.

You may have broken,
had I known you then. Even
twenty-one years later,
knowing me, you break:
pounded heart, trust inked
out, splayed thoughts

and legs. But you garner
your own garden
—hard intelligence—
trap insects that sting
or bite and scatter them
away from you.

iii.

Hearing piss expelled,
too fucked up on a morning
easily said, beautiful;

too depressed
to fuck, horny
with withdrawal;

I desire the boatman,
am eager to pay
to not get wet

in a border that quenches
and frees me of quench.
Dribble breaking open

this day begs questions:
will I, how'll I,
stave off, or deny?

Are failed attempts
enough, enough
to be a paid-up fare?

iv.

That *łééchąą yázhí*, little ground shitter
—protector *shi kis*—
I gave his carcass my hope
for him to lap at the river,
wet his paws, and wait for me
to remind me of what I'd lost.

v.

After five years, abuse
lasted five, six, seven more.
Continual blackout
addiction and distance.

I think of that fucking mixed wolf,
hardly beyond a pup,
that taught me how to accept
you and myself; tightened

the connectors powering me
—anger focused joy—
my murder of night drained
down to battery or assault.

From this view on the river,
current arrives and leaves
us—reflects and envisions
the one, now, with the other.

Middle of the Desert

For the weight of your bones
my blood thinned. Yesterday,
the east-hefted sun dissipated
humid, empty air
in space comprised of space;
dehydrated cactus and dirt barren
to the idea that it's cold here, ever.
Nostalgia charmed
out of a hollow:
the feeling, failed duty.

To you, who I've departed, walking
carefully as hooves on rain-wet granite
or other slippery stones,
are there heights after plunging
from which you'll never rise? Neither of us
is yet dead. But when I go before you
refer to me as *he* or the Diné one—
don't ever name. This voltage
wanting to hold you
when there is no ground.

Go to your home, the one you've made.
Ours that's gone. Rest in yourself and job.
If ever an earthquake or small tornado
hits again, pound
loosened nails back, clean and tape cracks,
prep for texture. If left without power
or light, trust an electrician who knows
luminaries guide only
when there are trees
or buildings to shine on.

Absent from this desert: stacks of bricks
that need to be re-pointed,
leaden Victorian glass unable to hold heat,
and roofs that connect every house
trading mold, alternating leaks.
Yesterday gone, the sun lifts off
your bones; barren weight
and humid dirt
caught me cut
short, saying

Troubleshooting

She wasn't better off to drive—weave
this paved city's grid, to lie together only,
and promise on waking to search our emptiness
                              for a way.

We never made it to our beds, but hurried
to her backseat, improvised the friction of our thighs,
and asked blow why whiskey, morning after,
                              claims forgiveness.

I'm addicted to her, an inversion—one open
neutral where current can't return through—
the potential to *yes*, home together, pleasure and arc
                              off each other.

Arc Flash

The stars went off and on, as if wired
by to-hell-with-it electricians
tired of lighting scrap-patched houses
connected by threads of predawn smoke
to invisible weavings in the sky.
Dim questions and silent answers.
Cattle, gaunt and wanting, grazed
between weeds across the valley,
interrogated the dirt of wash and creek.
How long since you've been clay after rain?

Startled awake at midnight and
under influence I sought my car
to kill the soft snores beside me.
Hauled ass out of urban desert decay
to sandstone cliffs, five hours away,
where centuries of wind
and more recent roadway gusts
have made a half-pipe of its base,
though not enough to topple
the edge of the mesa's level.

Hours from Phoenix, oasis
greedy and artificial, I needed Crystal,
my dad's home, and ceremony;
less familiar mountain tobacco.
Not to guide my spirit,
used to mornings being lit,
but to remind my tongue of blood;
cold coffee made by other men's
women who dispel me with smokes
from cheap packs set, within reach,

on their knees. Maybe they wish,
aside from my soon departure,
that I shared their danger: bastards

who make home, confinement and needs, hush.
I left and arrived months before the rainy season,
though cuts along the cliff face
over Crystal shimmered with mica.
Like stars burnt out taking eons
to reveal their absence
in myth-heavy constellations.

The sun risen
isn't for me,
cattle being herded,
or darkness in the room
I left to wake alone.
Here, a few cars idle
without drivers,
warm up before the workday
while smoke from houses vanishes
and releases the night sky.

Red Dirt

I work to be more than roots fed
through days of heat and dust

—evaporating into a brittle husk,
withdrawn and left as only remains.

Whether stirred out by force or removed
in mechanic iron swoops, I'm simple—

passed over and dumped onto a pile
of old ground, turned up, open to the air.

Bound in earth pack, I release seeds,
my blood to be windblown and spread.

Straining from new foundation I reach
to hold all-else, settled, empty of breath.

Currents

Phoenix, Arizona

I.

Each new sun asks: be
no thing more than me,
have nothing beyond need

—send opened your whole
being, lifted face, arms spread.
Though only part of me

is blessed, a body exerted
after long hours, responsibility,
and the need to ease tremors.

———

The last of March's
welfare won't go past
the eighteenth, hunger pains

dull month to month.
We've burned the final
log from February's half-

cord; son's schoolbooks,
claimed lost, are enough
to get the fire going.

———

My youth wasn't warm enough
to stone prairie dogs,
skin and eat.

The drive past the flats
no longer makes instant
noodles cheaper.

Mornings blind when throats throw
heat—stutter steps skid linoleum.
Untouched eggs feed me, forget me.

II.

Mom's a woman with
red skin and long receipts,
an aluminum façade

of sparkle-talk and sheen.
Measuring steps: easy win,
sudden guess.

Sissy boys
tear and candy don't
take care.

————

There isn't a nickel
in any cushion—
skeletal-hair remains

collect all over.
Red drips redder
than my skin,

redder than swallowed
embarrassment,
than slap—freezing feet.

————

A dark hall's corner,
a damask of lines,
the call-to mom uses,

telling me I don't add up.
I penguin-walk and cross
feet. In grass I pull

my knees up;
still, the grass
grows toward me.

III.

The coin-fare for
a crosstown bus a rosary
for time on my own.

Slow approach on
the upcoming stop, a heavy
let, a stiffened step

on concrete
right-angled silhouettes
the butane flame dawn.

———

The water's
hot and
there is light:

the home
encloses a
son lost

until 6:30 brings
noise of traffic
delays and brewing.

———

I get
little out
of this,

pay is ungrateful,
I eat little—
my eyes bulge.

I don't know
the woman
letting time slip.

The Occasion to Wake Wind

i.

Struck cold by morning sun, the decomposed
crumble in rows of upturned earth.
       Failure's given to
the toiler, who keeps earning less than promised.
       Drought these months,
unfed tributaries, nourishment tilled dirt.
       None of it's right—
       work, now, disappeared.

ii.

He stick-frames nightmares, after spring and warmth,
into a house he'll never own; one mansion, mosaic.
       Inside, what assaults
him is abstracted—mother serving
       rusted pennies, jagged
from reckless use. Screams, though the edges aren't
       real: only piss
       relieves sweat.

iii.

       All he does
       is plan how
to move quick, not rush to the place
       where his people are sent.
A moonless, sunless pitch burning fast
       and heavy—dried fields.
Heat waves blurring memory and trauma of seasons
when thirst was a silence, kept, only to crack.

Division

una polvareda grande
snaps the weak
points of mesquite,

fells moth egg-
filled saguaros—

divots across the desert
await gusts,
season's last rainfall

———

esta ciudad slick
with engine oil
heated on asphalt

beneath *las nubes*
negras y cautelares

this city's ashes
not of death
but movement

———

defying being bound
those who pray
para el norte

against shallow-rooted
keepers of the gate

find reprieve in
jugs left out—
throats eased

———

brownshirt bruisers
and local locos
gun up to get-*it*-done

Grounding

Crepúsculo,
una serpiente de polvo

—vans of *la migra*—

summoned by *contratistas*
cobardes who anticipate

a crack, irresolute
of its path.

Sin necesidad de
herramientas
curb-plucked workers

walked barefoot
through *cemento frió*

and floated suave
the curing surface.

Now they sit *encadenado*
y se preguntan

if they'll receive water
para lavar la roca

hardening around their feet.

Electricity

The morning roundup's
a current leaking to earth
without interruption or fault.

Above busted street lights the sun
buzzes to a cuffed line of deportees;
the sheriff's imbalanced authority.

Any laborer gathered for a tear-out
agrees the pleasure of opening walls
is the view of what's no longer behind.

The restrained motion of a body caught
within a fence run between language
is a union of shock and memory.

If Nothing, the Land

i. the toughest sheriff in the world

There is no other bad than what I say's bad.
It's tough-living on this land. Miles of desert,
undeveloped; the interstates, mostly unmanned,
are threads unspooled down broad hallways.
Beyond their edge the space is *dead*,
a rogue trailer or redskin reservation.
Backward problems
of methamphetamine and rape. Those doors

have their own police, their own dumb justice.
I concern my posse with invasion. Paperless
beaners. Rust that ruins a polish.
Inedible animals do no man any good
until buried to cease the flies and stink.

ii. flock of Seagals

If not thousands then millions of hours
I've played *bang-bang*; nabbed bad guy
brownies in kung-fu-grip shoot-'em-ups.
Who's better fit to patrol kids in tiny pants
than a convicted man? Limits,
like borders, stretch thin and tear. If anyone
can get a gun then shouldn't everyone
have one at the ready? Like in the glory days:

a roundup of savages, spics, and spooks out
to devalue our kids, good at killing their own.
I learned from watching birds nestled within
cacti: though there might be many, a single bird
more makes another cavity, an eventual collapse.

iii. come mierda para el desayuno

Chickens dismantle, like pit crews can
a vehicle, scorpions quickly.
Urged forward by pickers the hens bob
and amble over fallen oranges, bruised grapefruit;
seek pincers, stingers, exoskeletons;
their work urgent and efficient.
Back at the coop, stubborn roosters fight,
bloody, and unfeather each other

until the losers peck frail chicks from the clutch,
strew limp bodies beneath the florescent light.
The hens return, squawk and circle the carcasses,
until the migrants transfer them in sacks
meant for citrus to anonymous holes on the land.

A Structure in Parts

Quiet hours since dawn; casings cooled
      on pedestrian empty
      streets, dried with blood. The ghosted,
summoned by the sun, rise with dew to hear
      a photographer
murmur over beads, undulate prayer. Witnesses
lock themselves in against the traffic of trafficking.

A crew of homeless lug buckets of water,
      rinse down the storm drains, pools
      of pomegranate seeds
spilled from the ashen limbs cut from men.
      Unable shooters sent
to return with bodies on their guns. Though
begged, God has abandoned this town, others like it.

A coroner offers the obvious—
      full-leafed trees collapse in
      winter. A sergeant reads
cardboard jammed in the gouge of a lamp post.
      Manda los hombres.
Mantenga las cabezas. Here,
beyond the wall of abyss.

Hwéeldi

'Aak'ee
takes the last
'iiná.

'Ats'íís
crumpled on
nahasdzáán;

dineh bikágí
wants off its
'ats'in.

Gather *dii bąłi dóó*
bee'eldǫǫ bik'a'—
leave *łíeshłibaha.*

Na'zid dóó do'oodláą nahjį' adiilił
with corpses—
dabii'izhi baadiyinah.

Otoñal

errant primavera
son las palabras I give *nahasdzáán*
ensombrecido por nahattin

shikee' yaagi
it is
bii'hatts'aa'

las conchas de tééh tsisteł
filled *con*
tséko' dóó łeetsoh

ahora el viento
es tsó pero
doo níyol tsó da

esta vida es el trabajo
béésh átts'ózí dóó béésh tó bii' daníligíí
hazhó'ógo adiilił

Bini' Anit'ą́ą́ Ts'ósí

Opiate evening
moths bump
artificial flame.

I'm undone.
Prayer I prayed
quieter than click

of pharmies
ready to din
coming memory.

Shiyi'sizíinii doo bi dziil du.
Shikéyah dóó shijóó,
shik'ijįį naałdas.

Estas palabras that fail
take *hózhǫ́*
to be pressed

under foot
like body
beneath wet clay.

Esta no es mi idioma
and neither this
dóó di'ah doo da.

Evening Beneath Dust

I'm blowing smoke, ill thoughts toward the shadows
        of old bungalows, built before dusk
        became an ember of ozone and smog:
the highway is smashed with too many glasses for me
        to drive east to my sister, who stays
with every light on, so no uncertainty of the darkness
                can reach her.

She sleeps days; the house's high-ceilings incubate her
        while the sun guards the windows,
        doors, and closets. Forces into the open—
a jealous deliverer whose only opportunity to affect
        comes on nights with no moon.
The prayers my sister recites calm, though hardly quell,
                like wafers and wine.

Thoughts of saviors from foreign lands where boundaries,
        like imagined barriers bisecting an ocean,
        summon the idea: god or creator?
My sister calls our mother and father, once, to ask if the *ch'íídis*
        of our Diné history can be translated
into demons listed in a goetia. They know that any grow
                from love's demise.

So when I call her finally, after hours walking avenues
        of proposed guilt, it's not her I hear, but
        voicemail. I say this: Old Abraham,
the sheep of subservience, denied God, Isaac, or was it
        god denied God? Abe's blade made domestic,
he skinned a bush caught ibex. Offered it burnt. His boy
                ignited the sticks

of the alter-pyre he assembled, hungered at what wasn't
        his to eat. Isaac spent two-hundred years
     at the pitch end of wells, digging water.
His name, laughter-fits when nothing funny was done.
        Let's assume angels tickled him.
Why consider drugs, bipolarity, or a curse? He'd been
                    divined already.

It's lonely in the thirst of the sun, in the drowning of a well.
        The silhouettes in the houses around you
     will dance on occasion. It might not be
a two-step or waltz. But a bad lamp, some faulty wiring,
        a violent flicker that gets you worried.
Not knowing, *shideezhí*, is an unwanted voltage. A flood,
                a current engulfing you.

Baptism for the Dead

don't take my name to the water
a soul with no body to enter

the dead don't share skin with
the living—no conduit between

don't set me in afterlife
my name is my body

Nuestro Señor el Desollado:
Acrylic on Canvas: Paul Pletka: 2004

the man in the middle

Here's *your* Our Lord hung
with slipknots
from a pressure-treated cross

stenciled with grape vines
untended and unpicked
that await mash and ferment

into the drinkable blood
of El Señor. Xipe Totec
grows beneath the flesh

of an offered man, some bearded
born-again of Spanish
descent, playing the *passioned* Christ.

His face gone slack sooner
than those with food
and work, though not as tired,

hard failed as Indio peasants
dying under a deity
that makes rot and ash into

seasons, not blood to wine.
I'm one who'll eat
and certainly drink just as soon

as the man is cut down, removes
his disguise, and
the damned cross is put away.

the purple and gold cape

A stepladder is a precaution,
but not necessary.

Could stand on a couple milk crates,
untie the exhausted volunteer,
then strip and repaint the cross.

Man doesn't know work until he's met
with resistance and God

telling him to steady, right himself like
drunks reciting boleros

after failed one-night stands. Lost
in darkness, really just unlit paths
or sidewalks (not even an alley),

a guy will have to prove love or faith
—assuaged like Abraham—

renounce, give over offspring. Or vanquish
some foe: substance, heathen

empathy, or fine things that tempt.
Women are *fine things* and need
correcting. Especially if their skin

is soil rich and exotic. Gold and Gold trump
their worth.

Meaning that their prayers mean nil:
body, blood, too.

The land, the earth accepts severed
limbs and heads. Even char and ash.
In the end is the end. That's where

flags and riches matter. The kingdom, the gates,
and the master.

el hombre

Sure the *sangre* was real. What wasn't
came from *una cerda*.

Slaughtered a few days before La Cuaresma.
It smelled rancid

como la mierda that's been eaten and shit
out again. The face

I wore? *Era el rostro de mi hermano.*
What I mean is that

it came from off *his* head. We're not twins
you see, not even close

en los años. As far apart as we are in age
was about as long as

I hadn't seen him. *Nuestro madre* agreed
to this spectacle after

the narcos found him decapitated *en la calle*
among a dozen others.

The priests, Maya deity actors, and shamans
have methods against flesh

decaying completely or turning to leather.
That fucking thing,

mi hermanito's face, I mean, it still smelled
like him. It was no big deal.

I was it, it was me.

shepherd on the scarlet banner who carries
a lamb and cross made from sticks

Guy's robes are clean so they must have been a gift.
Royal blue wrapped at his waist, peach draped
over his shoulders. He's got no flock, though.

The lamb he carries: dinner. He's come off
mesas north of the valley, green already,
has allowed the lamb to graze and shit.

The contents of its stomach and intestines
will need little cleaning. Easy washing
makes the eating taste less like the ignorant

animal's food. Fresh wool is what this shepherd
of one needs. He looks like too much death:
rank and tattered skin he wears, cumbersome.

Nothing renewing or rejuvenating about this
asshole. A rejected reaper Christ with
huffer-glazed eyes and a methed-out mouth.

Too bad paintings or pictures can't, don't speak.
Sure his story's good. Better than any beggar's
outside a center city McDonald's. Even if he is

the Second Coming, no one's going to believe him.
Ghosts don't eat, zombies do. So there's bound
to be some zealot who'll gladly take his head.

unrecognized statue of a woman saint

Well, at least, someone bothered
to touch up the painted flowers
on my skirt and the ones coiled
around the sanctuary pillars.

They've, them, whoever, stuck a wig
on my head. Usually, a shawl hoods
my bucolic features. Farm girl, I hear
whispered from the nave. *Fea.* Today

real gardenias arc out before my feet.
So nice. They'll die, rot in a matter
of days; become something pretty
pressed in a book, hung off a hook.

The drapes that connect the altar
to the assembled were kept open.
Who could stand the crimson behind
the crucifixion of an already dead man?

All those prayers, all those laments?

the kneeling dama & girl

We're criers say the men,
an expected shrill
that's needed. Comforting

lament—call it a dirge
and it sounds nicer,
cultured. Mourning

is heavy fear deep within
the body. *Our* bodies:
a feeling, emotion, a trial.

Most of the sectioned rooms get no sun at all;
    strange evidence of the architect's knowing
        nada of what his container will hold.

      High rectangle windows and ones elongated
    in the corners offer natural light, though if
the *sol* or *estrellas* darken there's no technician

to change them. Guy working hourly replaces bulbs,
    troubleshoots breakers. Such are the conditions of on-loan
        work. Necessitates begging. The soul, like rain, requires a choir

      yowling the absence of crops and the slow plop of droplets
    that transform into sudden floods and bruising hail,
the *here you go* shushing wails. These days, donors

commission creators, label any genesis sacred. So, storm
    walls of darkness and dust have become useless emotional
        offerings. Blood is what's wanted. Churches raised from ground

      where the natives have suffered. Look and pay attention.
    The fanciful god and heaven haven't let go. Anyway,
we fear the indigenous. Not the worship of ourselves.

xipe totec

I'm no cairn vulture's circle.
Could say
I straddle birth and passing.

Bleeding men are what grow
the harvests
for me—for you, with you.

Some, they scream and cry.
Drink Christ's
blood. In frenzy, all forget

that the reason *His* life spilt
across *begat*
after begat was remembrance

of your pitiful life: sorry-ass sins.
Only earth
is more than me—greater yet

than you and *Him*. An entity for war,
celebration of
the judged, enemy, and heathen.

The celebration's a fraud, in the
pure and holy
sense. Look at the crowd.

I'm the small man whose kin
is missing;
a shawl warming an old woman;

the prayer, the prayed-to; the offering
and the offered;
the bent back and the harvest.

Notes

This collection is influenced by the stories, ideologies, and myths of various religious, mystic, and gnostic texts, primarily, the *Diné Bahane'* as told to me by family members and medicine people, as well as the written translation done by Peter G. Zolbrod, *The Holy Bible* (King James Version), *The Book of Mormon*, *The Satanic Bible*, and *T.A.Z.: The Temporary Autonomous Zone, Ontological Terrorism, Poetic Terrorism*, among others. Readers may benefit from a close read of any of these texts.

Breach

The myth of Jonah and the Whale has always fascinated me, especially as I witnessed Humpbacks breaching and swimming in Sitka Sound during the time I worked construction in Sitka, Alaska. Jonah's tomb was reduced to ashes and rubble on July 24, 2016, in Mosul, Iraq, by the Islamic State.

Ko' dóó łeeschch'iih

The title of the poem translates from the Diné Bizaad as "Fire and Ashes."

The first sentence in the first line of the fifth stanza, "It's the shape I'm," is taken from track three, "The Sinking Belle (Blue Sheep)," from the Boris and Sunn O))) collaborative album *Altar*, released October 31, 2006, through Southern Lord Records.

Hydrolysis

I.

As of 2015, 32 percent of all homes on the Navajo Nation lack electricity, 31 percent lack plumbing, 38 percent lack water services, 86 percent lack natural gas, and 60 percent lack telephone services.

There are more than 1,200 abandoned mines on Diné Bikéyah emitting gamma rays, poisoning soil, air, earth, and water sources. War is profit. War is fear. War is contamination. War is white and yellow cake.

II.

The Indian Student Placement Program (originally called the Lamanite Student Placement Program) spanned from 1947 to 2000 with an estimated 40,000 participants from 60 tribes across the United States and Canada.

Mormon mythology puts forth a narrative that suggests America's Indigenous peoples fled Israel in 600 B.C. and settled into two groups: the Nephites:

righteous and civilized; the Lamanites, savage and bloodthirsty, with hardened hearts, cursed by God with dark skin that made them loathsome. The Mormon Church considers it a sacred obligation to convert and redeem indigenous peoples, for we are "chosen."

For what is a soul but the idea of your eternal being beyond, perhaps, heaven and earth?

As with any oppressive system of assimilation a divide, a bipolarity was created. Those skinned of, or having shed, their indigenous traditions and roots for white culture and Mormon mythology, and those who seek reclamation, return.

III.

- Naayéé'neizghání: slayer of alien gods
- Tóbájíshchíní: born for water

The hero twins are the sons of Asdzą́ą́ Nádleehé (Changing Woman) and Jóhonaa'éí (the sun). They journeyed to destroy the foreign gods and monsters killing our people sometime after the emergence from The Third World into The Fourth World.

Cedar can be burned and used to cleanse one's being of needy spirits after a burial or death occurs. It can be used in prayer.

This Side of the River

It should be noted that this is a love poem as told to Charon.

iv.

- *łééchąą yázhí*: puppy
- *shi kis*: my friend

Arc Flash

A type of arc fault and explosion that results from low voltage-current ratio connection that travels through air to ground or another phase in an electrical system.

Red Dirt

This poem is dedicated to my early mentor and friend Jim Simmerman (March 5, 1952 – June 29, 2006) whom I studied with at Northern Arizona University.

Currents

The poem opens with a version of a prayer, or offering of corn pollen, done at sunrise in Diné tradition and knowing. It's my prayer/offering, and I share it with you.

"The sun is new each day." Heraclitus.

Division

- *una polvareda grande*: a large cloud of dust
- *esta ciudad*: this city
- *las nubes*: clouds
- *negras y cautelares*: black and cautionary
- *para el norte*: for the north
- locos: crazies

Grounding

- *crepúsculo*: twilight
- *una serpiente de polvo*: a serpent of dust
- *la migra*: immigration
- *contratistas / cobardes*: cowardly contractors
- *sin necesidad de herramientas*: without tools
- *cemento frió*: cold cement
- suave: smooth
- *encadenado*: chained
- *y se preguntan*: and they ask
- *para lavar la roca*: to wash the rock

If Nothing, the Land

A triptych in the voices of a criminal and unfit Maricopa County Sheriff Joe Arpaio, a washed-up-actor and pretend-lawman Steven Seagal, and a racist governor Jan Brewer (2009-2015), affectionately known as the "Crypt Keeper," an anthology television series host. In 2011, Brewer published *Scorpions for Breakfast: My Fight Against Special Interests, Liberal Media, and Cynical Politicos to Secure America's Border* with Broadside Books. It claims to be nonfiction.

- *come mierda para el desayuno*: eat shit for breakfast

A Structure in Parts

- *manda los hombres*: send the men
- *mantenga las cabezas*: keep the heads

Hwéeldi

Translates as *place of suffering or hardship* and is the Diné name for Bosque Redondo, a camp of Fort Sumner, where over 10,000 Diné and Mescalero Apaches were forcibly marched from 1864 to 1868. Along the more than 300 mile journey many died, were raped, and killed. The genocidal mentality, policy, and efficiency is claimed to have inspired Hilter and the Nazis who studied plans of Bosque Redondo when designing Jewish concentration camps. American innovation.

- *'aak'ee*: fall
- *'iiná*: life
- *'ats'íís*: bodies
- *nahasdzáán*: earth
- *dineh bikágí*: human skin
- *'ats'in*: bone
- *dii bali dóó*: blankets and
- *bee'eldǫǫ bik'a'*: bullets
- *łeshłibaha*: dust
- *na'zid dóó do'oodláą nahjį' adiilił*: bury fear and doubt
- *dabii'izhi baadiyinah*: forget those names

Otoñal

Translates as *autumn* or *autumnal* from the Spanish.

- *primavera*: spring
- *son las palabras*: are the words
- *nahasdzáán*: earth
- *ensombrecido por*: shadowed by
- *nahałtin*: rain
- *shikee' yaagi*: under my feet
- *bii'hałts'aa'*: hollow
- *las conchas de*: the shells of
- *tééh tsisteeł*: sea turtle
- *con*: with

- *tséko' dóó łeetsoh*: coal and uranium
- *ahora el viento*: now the wind
- *es*: is
- *tsó*: big
- *pero*: but
- *doo níyol tsó da*: not a tornado
- *esta vida es el trabajo*: this life is work
- *béésh átts'ózí dóó béésh tó bii' danílígíí*: wires and water pipes
- *hazhó'ógo adiilit*: do it carefully

Bini' Anit'ą́ą́ Ts'ósí

Translates as October from the Diné Bizaad. It is also the first day of the Diné calendar. The harvest.

- *shiyi'sizíinii doo bi dzííl da*: I have no soul
- *shikéyah dóó shijéí*: my country and my heart
- *shik'iijįį naałdas*: they crash down on me
- *hózhǫ́*: balance. Essentially the Diné ideology of existing within and with everything in the universe.
- *esta no es mi idioma*: this is not my language
- *dóó di'ah doo da*: and not this

Evening Beneath Dust

- *ch'íídis*: ghosts or evil spirits
- *shideezhí*: my little (younger) sister

Baptism for the Dead

A baptism performed for a deceased person vicariously through one who is living. Generally it is the deceased's relative who is baptized by proxy. The Mormon Church has held this practice as doctrine since 1840 and controversially performed baptisms for the dead for Jewish Holocaust victims as well as Hitler himself. A collection plate or tithe of souls, even the most wretched.

One of the taboos of Diné ideology and belief is that we don't speak the names of one that has passed, so as not to summon or disturb their spirit. Rather we refer to them descriptively or in terms of their relation to us or another person. Baptisms of the dead then are sacrilegious and disruptive.

Nuestro Señor el Desollado

This large triptych (Our Lord the Flayed One) is housed at the Phoenix Art Museum and is the work of neo-surrealist Paul Pletka, a self-taught painter. His work is deeply spiritual, surreal, heavily researched, and representative of Indigenous practice and belief. Xipe Totec has been depicted in the Codex Borgia, a ritual and divinatory manuscript that survived the purge of history and culture by Spanish conquistadors and priests.

the man in the middle

- Xipe Totec: (Our Lord the Flayed One) is the Aztec deity for life, death, and rebirth; god of agriculture, vegetation, the east, spring, gold and silversmiths, liberation, and the seasons.

el hombre

- *sangre*: blood
- *una cerda*: a pig
- La Cuaresma: Lent
- *como la mierda*: like shit
- *era el rostro de mi hermano*: it was my brother's face
- *en los años*: in years (age)
- *nuestro madre*: our mother
- *en la calle*: in the street
- *mi hermanito*: my little brother

BOJAN LOUIS is a member of the Navajo Nation—Naakai Dine'é; Ashiihí; Ta'neezahnii; Bilgáana. He is a poet, fiction writer, essayist, and poetry and production editor for *RED INK: An International Journal of Indigenous Literature, Arts, & Humanities,* and the author of the nonfiction chapbook, *Troubleshooting Silence in Arizona* (Guillotine, 2012). He has been a resident at the MacDowell Colony.

This book is set in Baskerville, Optima, and Zapfino.

CPSIA information can be obtained
at www.ICGtesting.com
Printed in the USA
LVHW09s0042160818
587148LV00001B/121/P